GOD MADE ALL SORTS OF WILD ANIMALS, LIVESTOCK, AND SMALL ANIMALS.

EACH WAS ABLE TO PRODUCE OFFSPRING OF THE SAME KIND.

THEN THE LORD GOD FORMED THE MAN FROM THE DUST OF THE GROUND.

HE BREATHED THE BREATH OF LIFE INTO THE MAN'S NOSTRILS, AND THE MAN BECAME A LIVING PERSON.

THEN THE LORD GOD SAID " IT IS NOT GOOD FOR THE MAN TO BE ALONE".

THE SERPENT WAS THE SHREWDEST OF ALL WILD ANIMALS
THE LORD HAD MADE.

SO THE LORD GOD CAUSED THE MAN
TO FALL INTO A DEEP SLEEP.

THEN THE LORD MADE A WOMAN FROM
THE MAN'S RIB, AND HE BROUGHT HER TO THE MAN.

"DID GOD REALLY SAY YOU MUST NOT EAT THE FRUIT FROM ANY OF THE TREES IN THE GARDEN?".
F COURSE NOT, IT'S LY THE FRUIT FROM TREE IN THE MIDDLE THE GARDEN THAT WE E NOT ALLOWED TO EAT".
"GOD KNOWS THAT YOUR EYES WILL BE OPENED AS SOON AS YOU EAT IT, AND YOU WILL BE LIKE GOD, KNOWING BOTH GOOD AND EVIL."
THE WOMAN WAS DECEIVED BY THE SERPENT, SO SHE REACHED AND TOOK A BITE OF THE FRUIT THAT LOOKED SO APPEALING.

AFTER THIS, IT LEAD TO THE BANISHMENT OF M[
AND WOMEN BECAUSE OF THEIR DISOBEDIENCE

THE LORD GOD PLACED CHERUBIM TO THE
EAST OF THE GARDEN CALLED EDEN.

THROUGHOUT THE EXTENT OF THEIR LIVES, ALL GOD COULD SEE WAS EVIL AND WICKEDNESS.

GOD HAD MERCY ON A MAN NAMED NOAH.

NOAH WAS THE ONLY BLAMELESS MAN ON EARTH, WHO HAD A CLOSE CONNECTION WITH GOD.

NOAH WAS THE FATHER OF THREE SONS NAMED SHEM, HAM, AND JAPHETH.

GOD WAS READY TO DESTROY EARTH AND ALL WHO LIVED ON IT.

HE TOLD NOAH TO BUILD A GIGANTIC ARK.

GOD GAVE HIM INSTRUCTIONS ON WHAT TO DO.

NOAH DID AS HE WAS TOLD.

GOD MADE A COVENANT WITH NOAH, AND ALLOWED HIM AND HIS FAMILY IN.

GOD INSTRUCTED NOAH TO TAKE PAIRS OF EVERY LIVING ANIMAL, MALE AND FEMALE.

AND THE DOORS OF THE ARK OPENED.

YEARS LATER..
THE LORD GOD HAD SENT ABRAHAM TO SACRIFICE HIS SON AS AN OFFERING TO HIM.
ABRAHAM A MAN THAT FOLLOWED GOD'S COMMANDS NO MATTER HOW HARD THEY WERE TO FOLLOW.
"WHERE ARE WE GOING?".
THE NEXT MORNING ABRAHAM GOT EVERYTHING READY AND CARRIED ALONG WITH ISSAC TO THE PLACE GOD TOLD HIM.

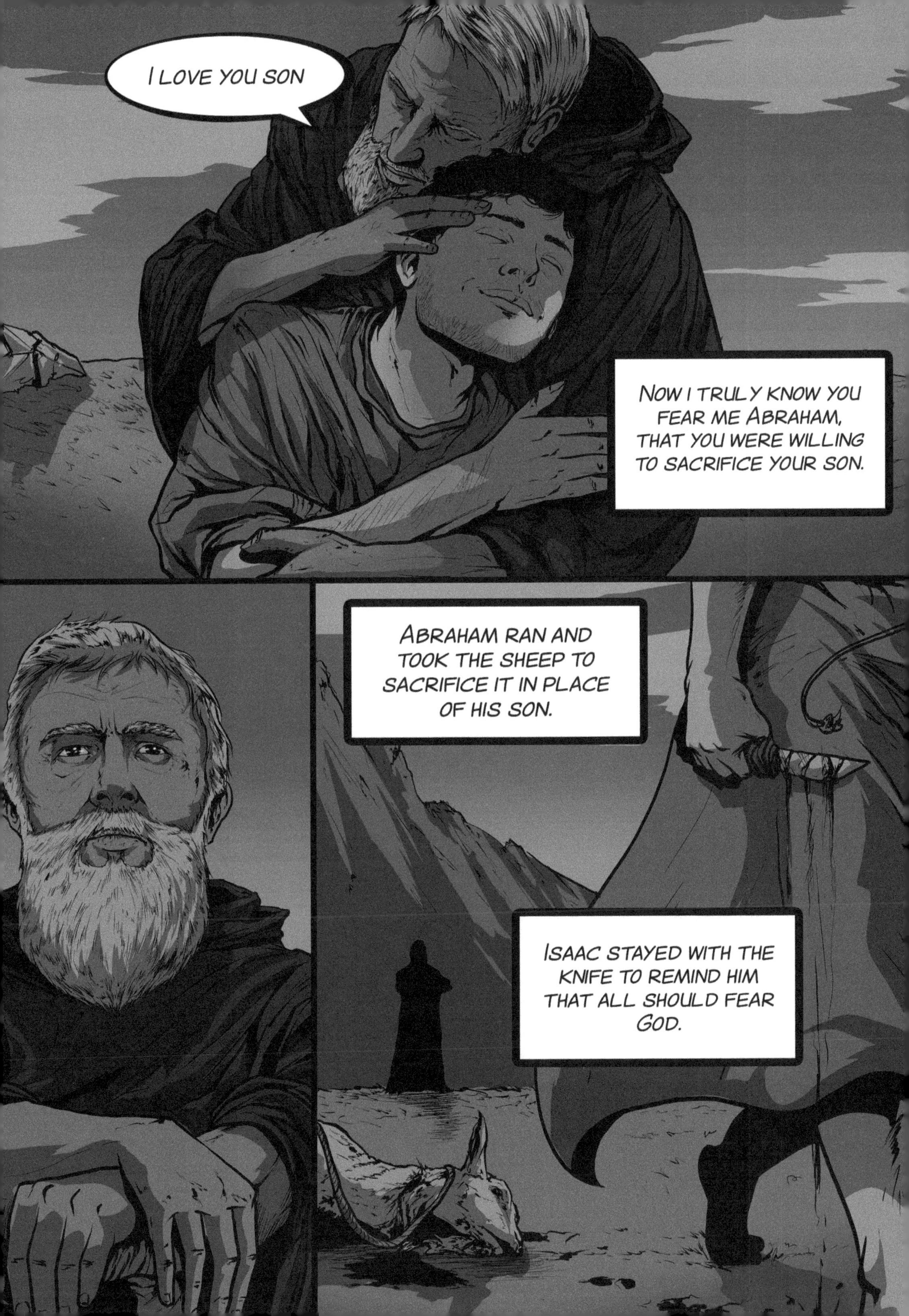
I LOVE YOU SON
NOW I TRULY KNOW YOU FEAR ME ABRAHAM, THAT YOU WERE WILLING TO SACRIFICE YOUR SON.
ABRAHAM RAN AND TOOK THE SHEEP TO SACRIFICE IT IN PLACE OF HIS SON.
ISAAC STAYED WITH THE KNIFE TO REMIND HIM THAT ALL SHOULD FEAR GOD.

JOSEPH AND HIS INTERPRETATION OF DREAMS.
" YOU WILL BE MY PERSONAL ATTENDANT".
"THANK YOU FOR TH OPPORTUNITY".
JOSEPH WAS SOLD TO A CAPTAIN CALLED POTIPHAR, AFTER BEING SOLD BY HIS BROTHERS.
JOSEPH WAS BROUGHT BACK TO PRISON BECAUSE HE WAS ACCUSED OF SEDUCING THE PHARAOH'S WIFE.
AND THIS IS WHERE IT ALL BEGAN...

THE CUP-BEARER, THE CHIEF BAKER, AND THEIR DREAMS.

WHEN THE CHIEF BAKER SAW HOW JOSEPH INTERPRETED THE DREAM, HE TOLD HIM HIS DREAM WHICH CONTAINED THREE PLATES OF VARIOUS PASTRIES, BUT BIRDS CAME AND ATE THE TOP PLATE.

THE CUP-BEARER HAD A DREAM WITH THREE VINES WHICH BLOSSOMED WITH A CLUSTERS OF GRAPES. E WAS THEN BACK WITH THE PHARAOH SQUEEZING THE GRAPES ONTO THE CUP.

DREAMING...
HE OPENED HIS EYES, CONFUSED OF WHAT HE HAD DREAMED.
WHAT DOES THIS MEAN?
THE TRANSLATION OF THE DREAMS.
JOSEPH EXPLAINED THAT IN THREE DAYS A CUP-BEARER WILL BE GIVEN HIS JOB BACK.
JOSEPH TOLD THE BAKER THAT IN THREE DAYS HE WAS GOING TO BE TAKEN BACK BUT EXECUTED ON A POLE TO BE PECKED BY BIRDS.
" PLEASE DON'T FORGET ABOUT ME".

SUDDENLY, EVERYTHING JOSEPH HAS SAID, CAME TRUE.

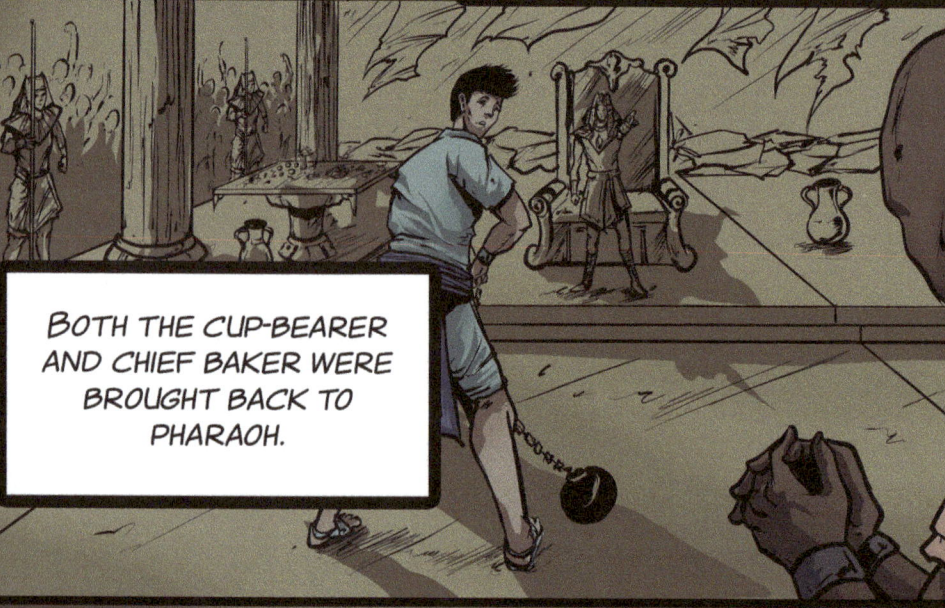

BOTH THE CUP-BEARER AND CHIEF BAKER WERE BROUGHT BACK TO PHARAOH.

BUT ONLY ONE WAS GIVEN MERCY.

"YOU ARE NOT WORTHY OF THIS JOB, SO YOU WILL BE EXECUTED".

AND EXECUTED HE WAS, JUST AS JOSEPH INTERPRETED.

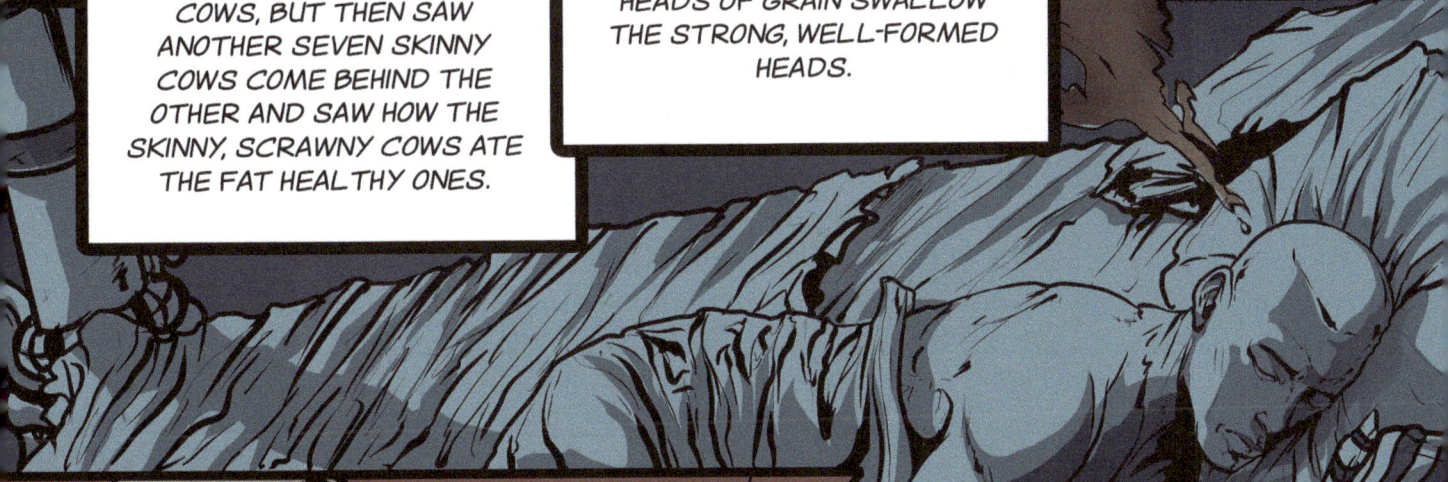

THE PHARAOH BECAME CONCERNED AND SENT TO LOOK FOR AN EXPLANATION OF WHAT THE DREAMS MEANT.

THE CUP-BEARER FINALLY REMEMBERED THAT THERE WAS A MAN NAMED JOSEPH WHO COULD INTERPRET DREAMS.

JOSEPH WAS BROUGHT BACK TO THE PHARAOH.

AND IT WAS THERE, THAT THE PHARAOH EXPLAINED HIS DREAM AND JOSEPH INTERPRETED WHAT IT MEANT.

The freedom of the Israelite
What is that burning?!
"Moses, Moses, do not come any closer. And remove your sandals, because you are standing on holy ground".
"I have heard the cries of my people, and I have come to save them"
"Moises go, you will lead my people out of Egypt".

THE NILE RIVER TURNED INTO BLOOD.

AHHH!

AND GOD SENT A TREMENDOUS HAILSTORM.

THEN ALL THE PEOPLE OF EGYPT WERE COVERED IN FESTERING BOILS.

AND IT WASN'T OVER YET...

THEN LOCUSTS STORMED ALL OVER THE LAND.

AND THEN THERE WAS DARKNESS.

SO THE ANGEL OF DEATH STRIKED THAT NIGHT.

"RUNNNN..."

SWOOOSSHHHHHH.....

THE FIRST BORNS WERE FOUND DEAD.

AND THE WATERS SPLIT

BUT THE PHARAOH WAS SO AMAZED HIS FACE WAS PRICELESS.

All Israelites were chased by Pharaoh's men
But the waters clashed back, and swept away Pharaoh's men
And the Lord Banished them into the sea.

AFTER WALKING FOR DAYS, THEY STOPPED AND MOSES WAS CALLED TO THE MOUNTAIN.

WHERE THE TEN COMMANDMENTS WERE GIVEN BY GOD.

AND THERE IT WAS..

THE FINGER OF GOD HAD CREATED THE TEN COMMANDMENTS.

THEN AARON BEGAN TO MELT ALL THE GOLD

HE SCULPTED A GOLDEN CALF WHO THEY WOULD SOON WORSHIP.

AND THEY ALL CELEBRATED

MOSES WAS ON HIS WAY BACK TO HIS PEOPLE

HE WAS BAFFLED TO SEE THE GOLDEN CALF AND THE ACTIONS OF HIS PEOPLE

MOSES SAW HIS PEOPLE AND BURNED WITH ANGER

HE THREW THE STONE TABLETS TO THE GROUND SHATTERING THEM

BIOGRAPHIES

Javier H. Ortiz

Is the founder and president of Supernesis Comics. He has written books for all ages: children, youth, and adults. He also travels around the world participating in conferences to help people to achieve their highest potential. He is the author of The Walking Word, Poor Christian and Rich Christian, and The Diary of Jom Junior books. Many of his readers have been positively impacted to make changes in the world around them. As an author his goal is to enrich others in every aspect of their lives. His most recent book is the Supernesis Comics Bible. During the creative process Javier stays true to his favorite slogan, "We love reality."

Jaime L. Villalba

Is an illustrator and colorists of Supernesis Comics Bible. At the young of 24 Jamie created his first animated motion comic series for Colombia called Butiman. It consisted of 24 episodes which was nominated for three prizes for India Catalina in 2014 and 2015. Jaime's career as an illustrator has progressed to large entertainment companies such as the Telecaribe, Caracol Television and Blue Radio Channels. Throughout the Latin American culture Jamie is one of the most sought out graphic design and digital illustration instructor.

In addition, Wacom Latam the largest graphic tablet company has chosen Jamie as their promoter and influencer of their brand.

www.ingramcontent.com/pod-product-compliance
Lightning Source LLC
Chambersburg PA
CBHW040258100426
42811CB00011B/1304